Schirmer's Library of Musical Classics

Vol. 424

JOHANN SEBASTIAN BACH

A COLLECTION OF
LITTLE PRELUDES AND FUGUES

PREPARATORY TO THE WELL-TEMPERED CLAVICHORD AND

INCLUDING

SIX LITTLE FUGUES

BY HIS SON

WILHELM FRIEDEMANN BACH

PROGRESSIVELY ARRANGED, FINGERED AND EDITED BY
G. BUONAMICI

ISBN 978-0-7935-5204-7

G. SCHIRMER, Inc.

DISTRIBUTED BY
HAL•LEONARD
CORPORATION
7777 W. BLUEMOUND RD. P.O. BOX 13819 MILWAUKEE, WI 53213

Printed in the U.S.A. by G. Schirmer, Inc.

PREFACE.

It has always seemed to me that young pianists who have not the advantage of some one to direct their studies seriously and systematically, generally attempt Bach's "Well-tempered Clavichord" too soon, and without due preparation.

I cannot explain this otherwise than by the absence of a preparatory school, or, I might say, of a preparatory volume, which it is my aim, in the following work, to furnish. It is much easier to work at a book conscientiously edited and containing all that is wanted, than to search for a fugue here and a fugue there, possibly very inaccurately edited, or with old-fashioned fingering and uncertain indications (if any).

These considerations led me to form the following collection, in which I have brought together a selection of small fugues (*Fughette*) which seem better suited to my purpose; and as only six of these (Nos. 3, 6, 7, 12, 16, 17) were preceded by a prelude, I have provided the rest with preludes; by this means, and by the regular alternation of major and minor keys, making my little volume more like the "Well-tempered Clavichord".

Not wishing to use preludes which already belonged to other compositions, I have employed Bach's own "Short Preludes". This is sufficient to defend me from the possible reproach, that any prelude is too short or too easy as compared with the fugue to which it is joined.

I have also to claim indulgence for the slight license taken in transposing preludes Nos. 5, 11, and 13 a tone, in order to adapt them to the keys of the fugues to which they are united; and, further, for having omitted the "repeats" in preludes Nos. 1, 5, and 8, and for having substituted notes (which are printed in small type) which serve in each case to join the first part to the second; thus giving that continuity and unity which are expected between a prelude and the fugue to which it belongs.

But, as the works of Bach with which I am acquainted do not present enough *Fughette*, sufficiently short and easy, to lend to my work the progressive character desired, I have ventured to insert six fugues (Nos. 1, 2, 5, 8, 9, 11) by his son Wilhelm Friedemann. The value of

these works, and the close relationship of the composers, authorize me in combining them without scruples,—a proceeding which might otherwise have appeared of very doubtful taste.

As regards fingering, I prefer to keep to the plan adopted by Czerny, which indicates, by figures written above or below the notes, with which hand they are to be played, rather than to the plan pursued by Bülow, Liszt, Tausig, and others, of writing nearly all the notes for the right hand on the upper staff, and those for the left on the lower. I prefer the former of these two plans because it better enables me to show the progression of the different parts, a point which I consider essential for young people whose eyes are not yet sufficiently trained to follow the progression of each separate part, if put before them in a less clear or apparently imperfect manner for convenience of execution. In short, I prefer that the pupil should incur some trouble to observe with which hand he is to play any given note, rather than to let him run the risk of overlooking or neglecting a theme, a phrase, or a part of one.

But, when this risk has ceased through his further progress, the second plan will be preferable, because more convenient. And, in fact, how could it be otherwise, since it has been adopted by the above-mentioned authorities?

It will be observed that the keys employed in this collection are all simple ones, not going beyond the limits of two sharps or three flats; but I do not think that this is a defect. The student who goes through this preparatory work is not yet able to grapple with the difficulty of intricate keys, and at the same time with all the other difficulties; and, besides puzzling him overmuch, it would lessen the possibility of his learning some of these works by heart, which it is most desirable he should do.

And, moreover, when a student has the wish and the power, what is to prevent him from transposing? In such a case the advantage would only be doubled, and I, hoping that there are many pupils who will attempt it, wish them all success.

GIUSEPPE BUONAMICI.

CONTENTS.

1. (D maj.) Preludio. — Andante. | Fughetta. — Allegretto. | Page 4.

2. (D min.) „ — Moderato. | „ — Andante mesto. | „ 8.

3. (G maj.) „ — Allegro. | „ — Allegretto. | „ 12.

4. (C min.) „ — Con moto. | „ — Moderato. | „ 16.

5. (Eb maj.) „ — Moderato. | „ — Allegro moderato. | „ 20.

6. (D min.) „ — Andante. | „ — Allegretto. | „ 24.

7. (F maj.) „ — Allegretto. | „ — Andante moderato. | „ 28.

8. (E min.) „ — Allegro. | „ — Andante espressivo. | „ 32.

9. (C maj.) „ — Allegro non troppo. | „ — Moderato. | „ 37.

10. (E min.) „ — Andantino con moto. | „ — Allegro moderato. | „ 40.

11. (Eb maj.) „ — Allegretto. | „ — Andante cantabile. | „ 44.

12. (A min.) „ — Moderato assai. | „ — Allegretto non troppo. | „ 48.

13. (C maj.) „ — Andante. | „ — Allegro. | „ 52.

14. (D min.) „ — Andante. | „ — Moderato. | „ 56.

15. (C maj.) „ — Allegro moderato. | „ — Allegro moderato. | „ 60.

16. (E min.) „ — Andantino. | „ — Allegro moderato. | „ 64.

17. (Eb maj.) „ — Allegro. | Fuga. — Moderato. | „ 70.

18. (A min.) „ — Allegro moderato. | „ — Allegro. | „ 78.

13212

I.
Preludio.

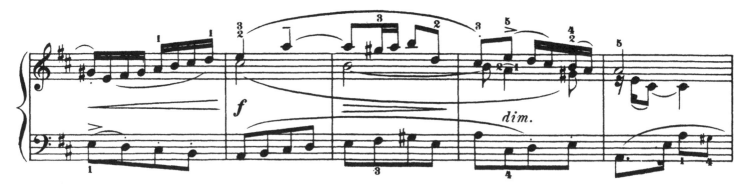

All the figures written *above* the notes (even if written on the lower staff) are to be taken by the right hand, and those *below* the notes (even if written on the upper staff) are to be taken by the left hand.

13212   Printed in the U.S.A. by G. Schirmer, Inc.

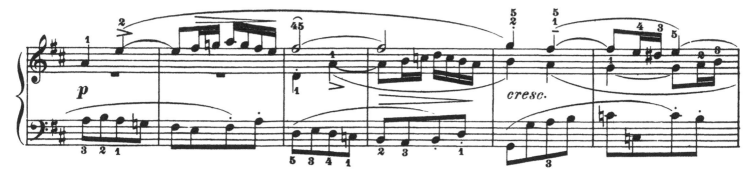

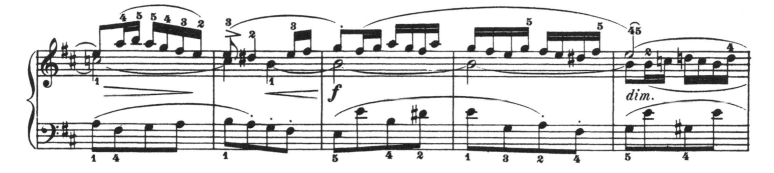

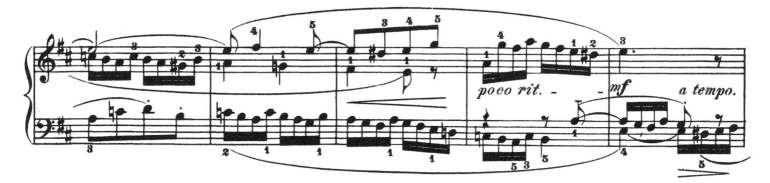

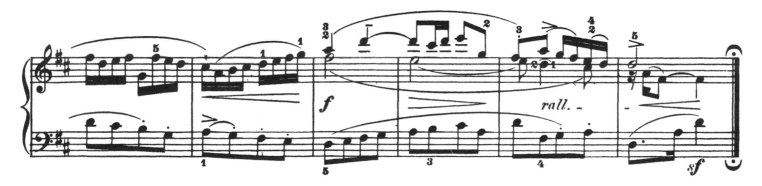

Fughetta.

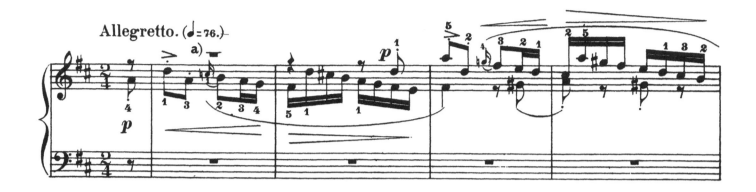

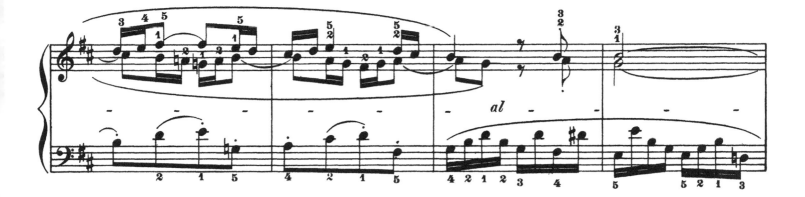

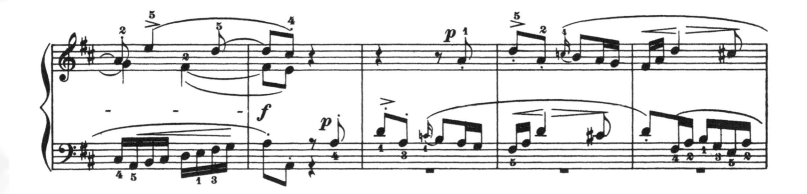

II.
Preludio.

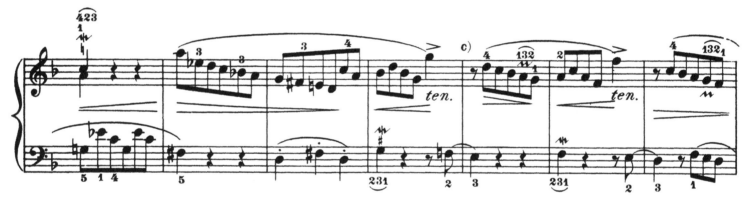

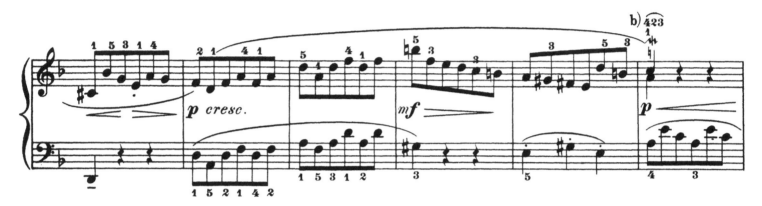

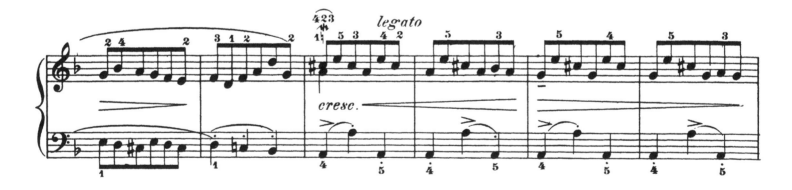

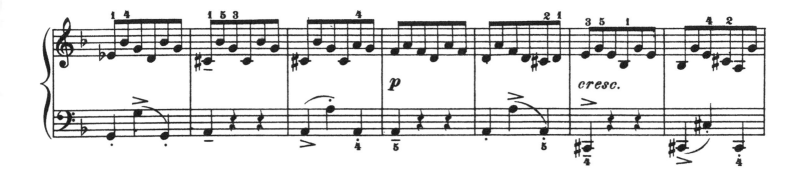

Fughetta.

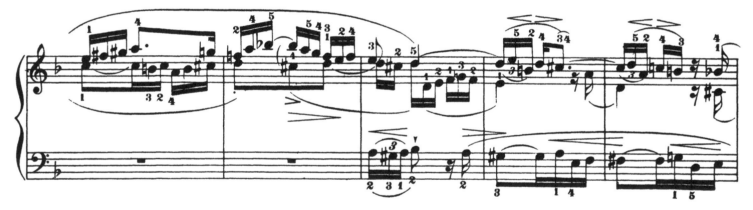

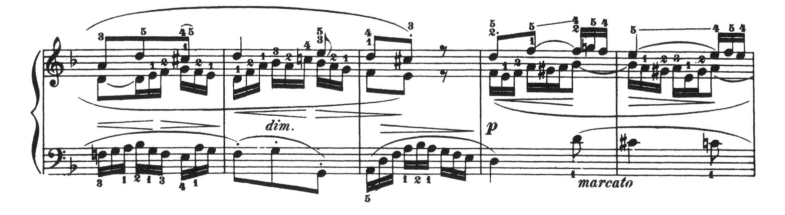

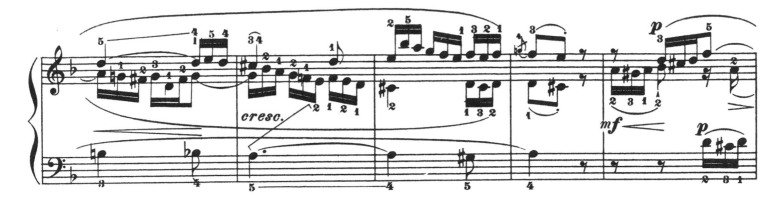

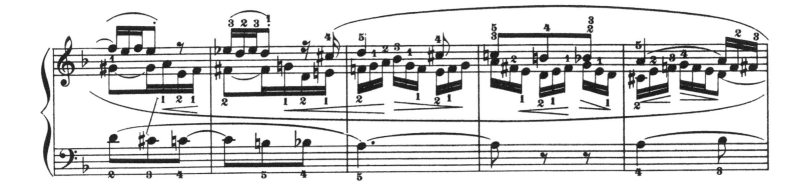

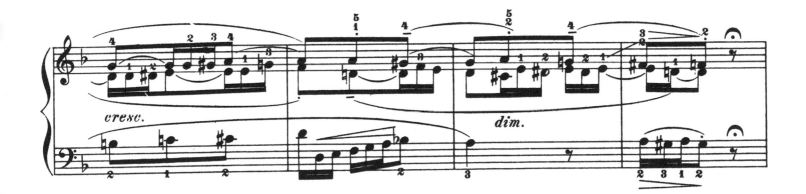

III.
Preludio.

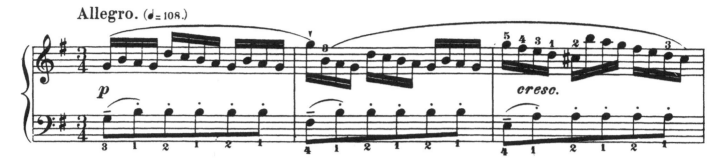

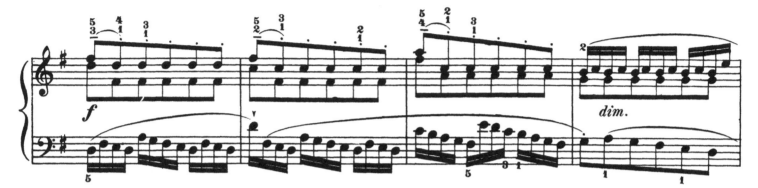

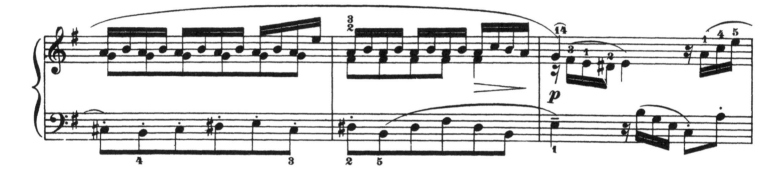

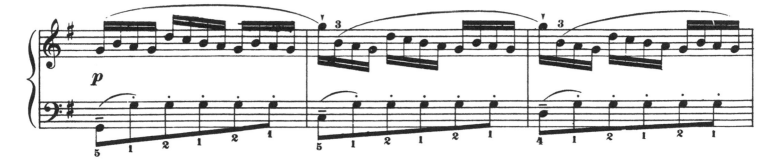

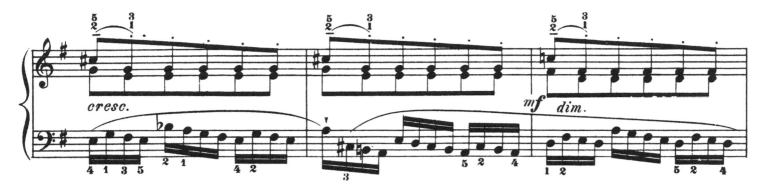

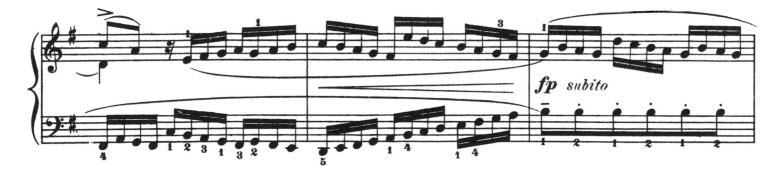

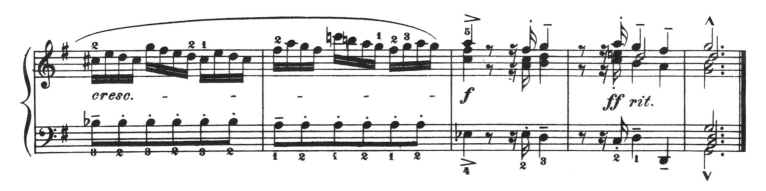

Fughetta.

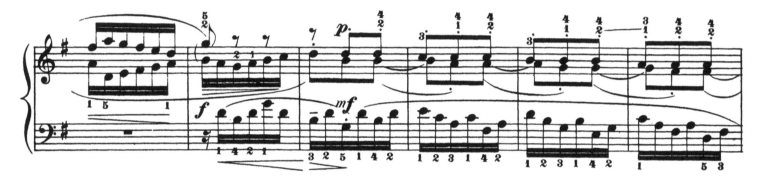

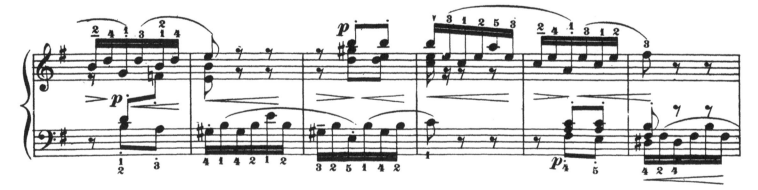

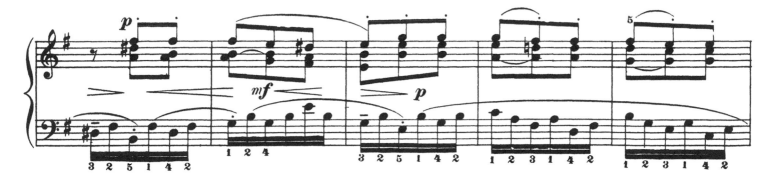

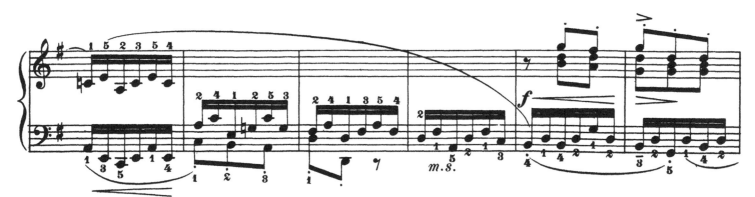

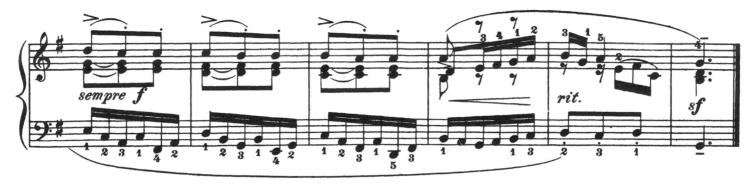

IV.
Preludio.

Con moto (♩=120)

Fughetta.

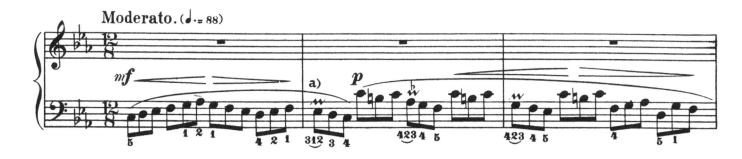

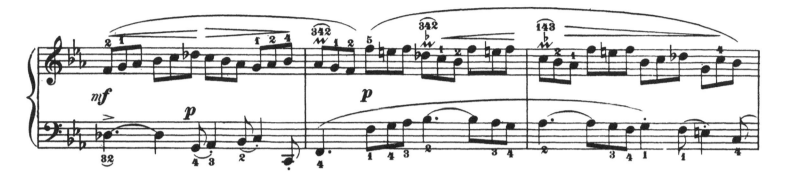

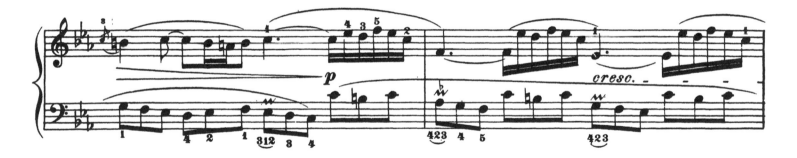

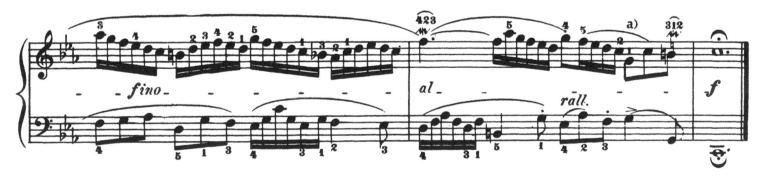

V.
Preludio.

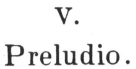

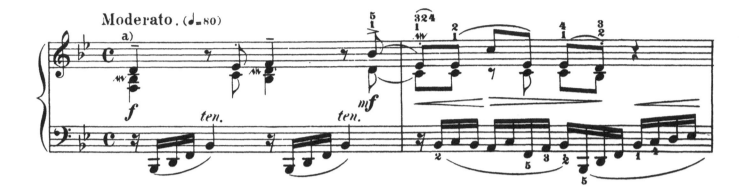

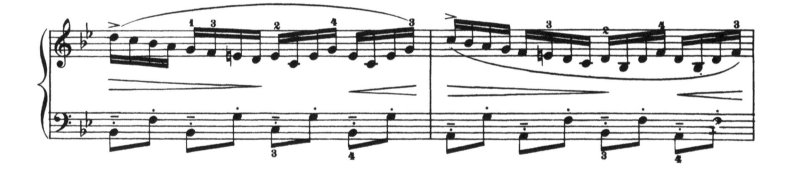

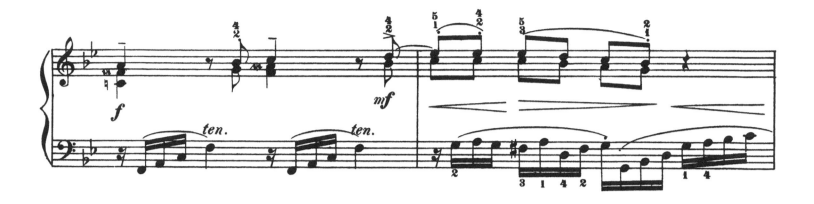

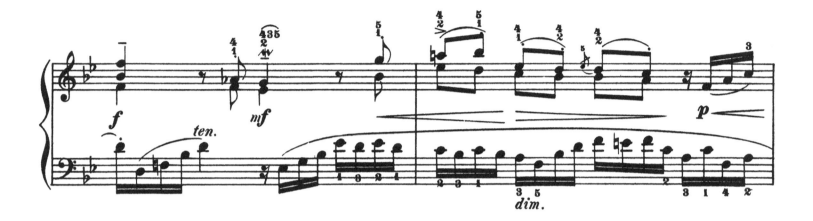

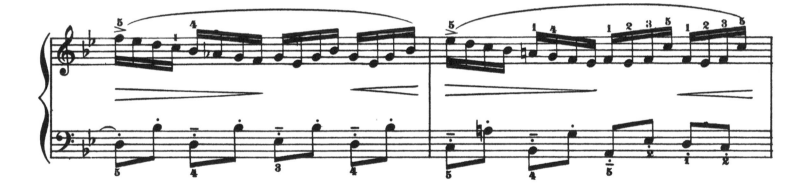

Fughetta.

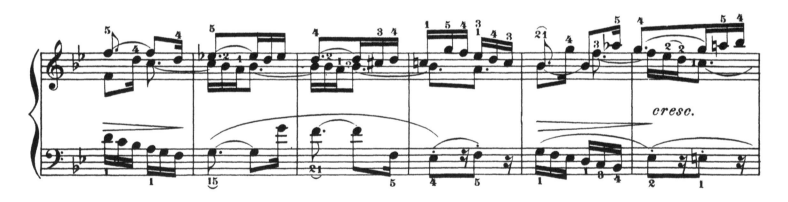

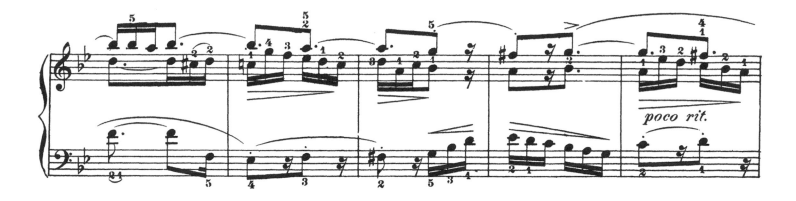

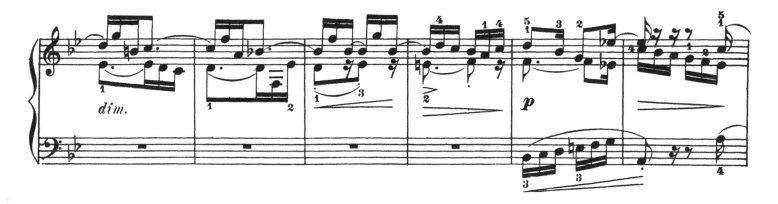

VI.
Preludio.

Andante. ($\quad$ = 60)

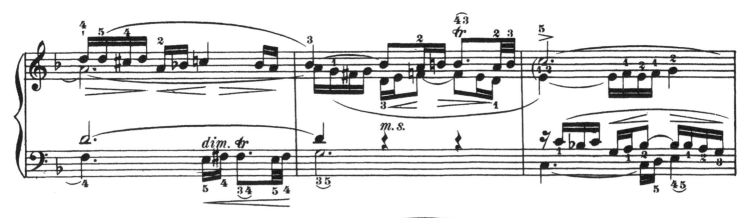

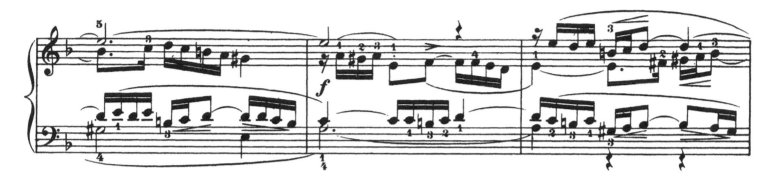

Fughetta.

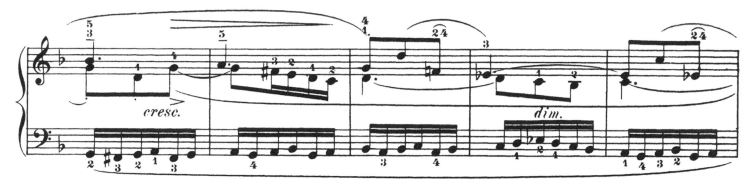

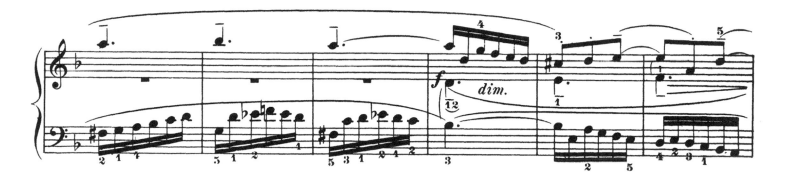

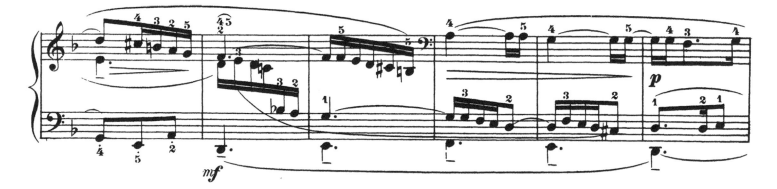

VII.
Preludio.

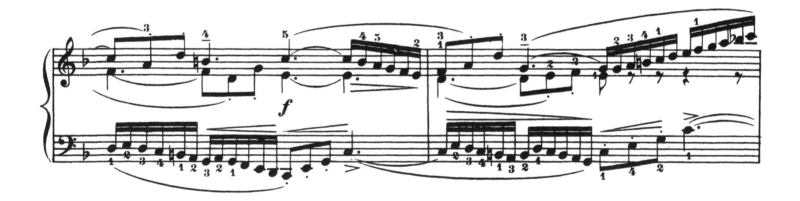

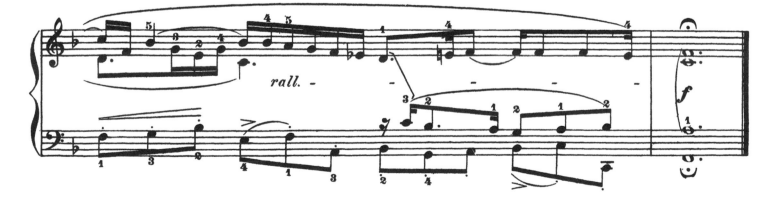

Fughetta.

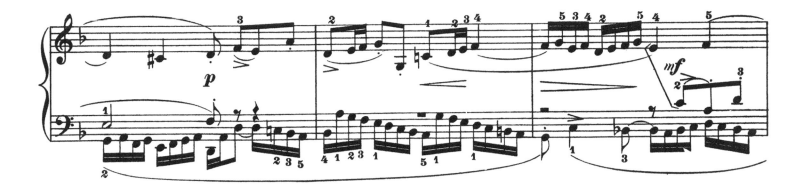

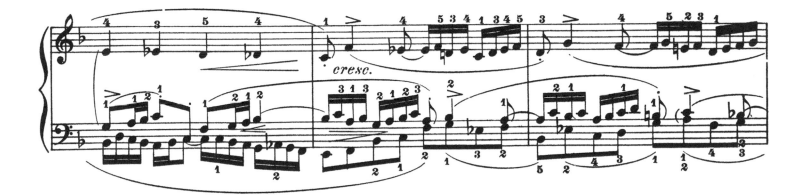

VIII.
Preludio.

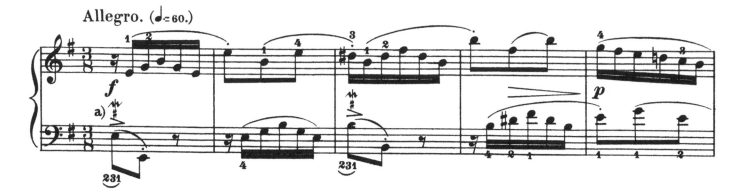

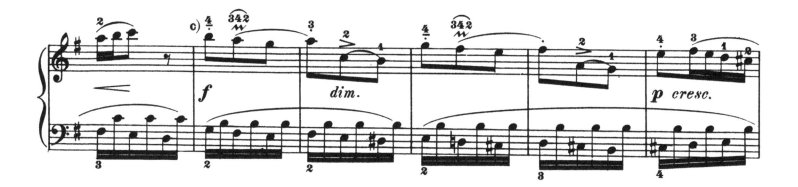

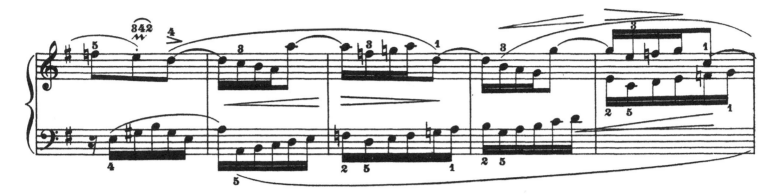

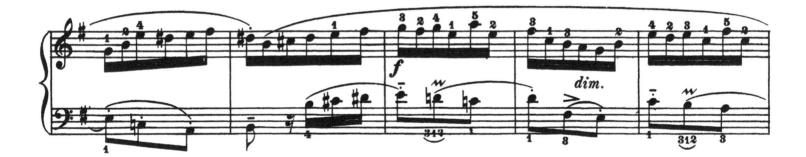

Fughetta.

Andantino espressivo. (♩.= 60.)
cantabile.

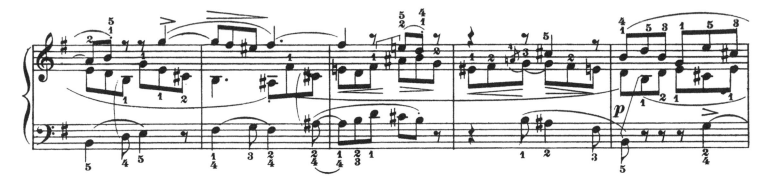

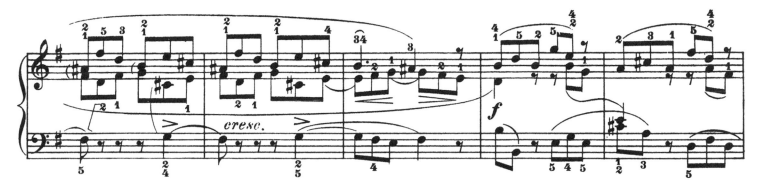

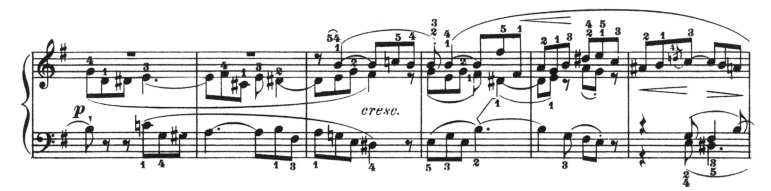

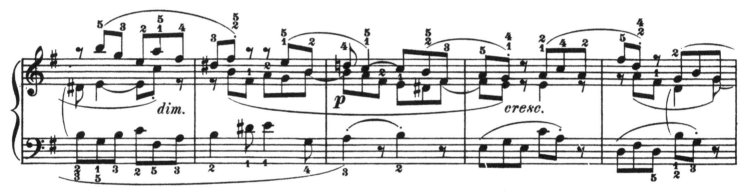

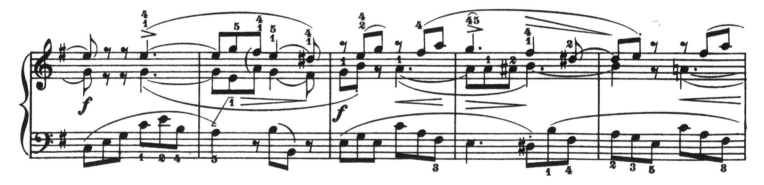

IX.
Preludio.

Allegro non troppo.(d = 88.)

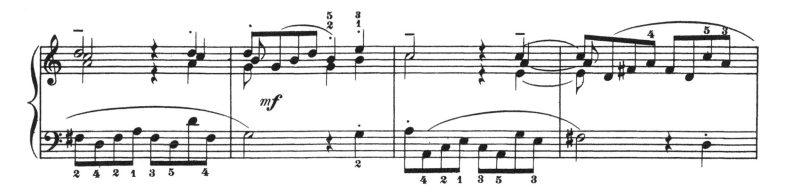

13212

Fughetta.

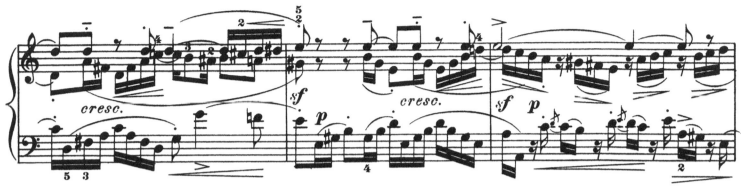

X.
Preludio.

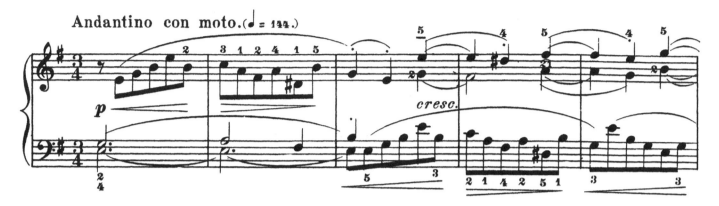

Fughetta.

Allegro moderato. (♩ = 88.)

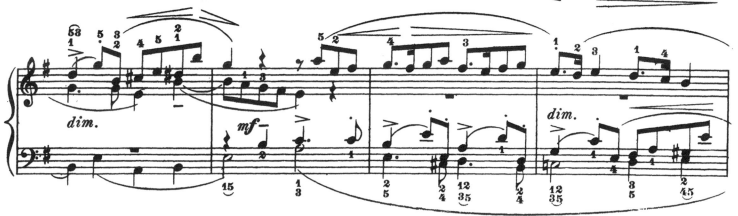

13212

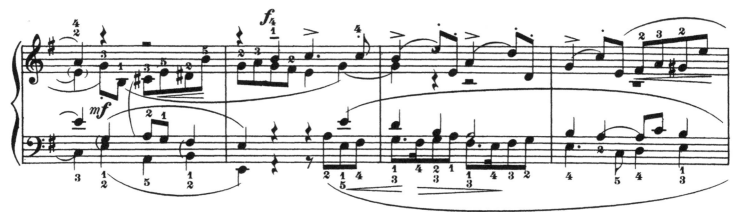

XI.
Preludio.

Allegretto. ($\quad$ = 108)

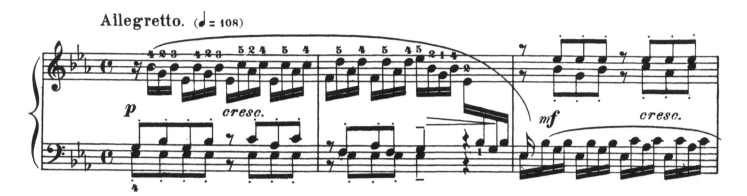

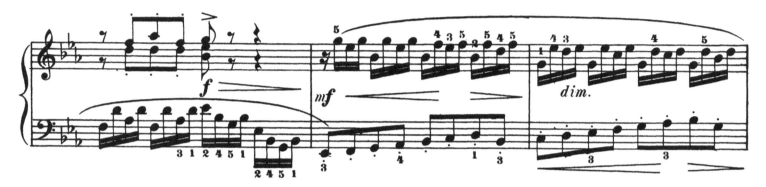

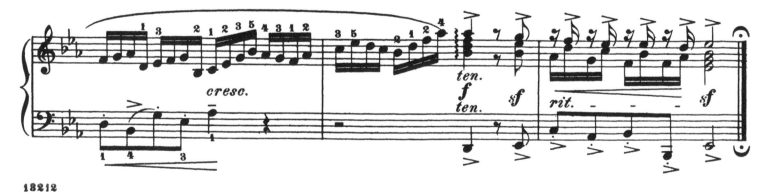

Fughetta.

Andante cantabile. ($\bullet$ = 120)

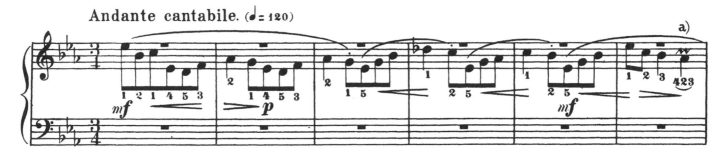

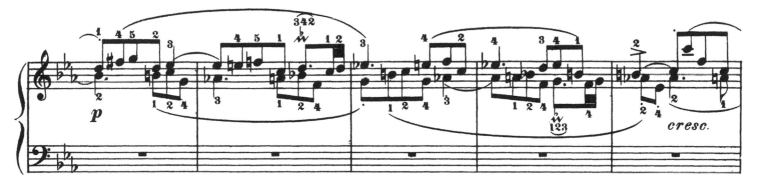

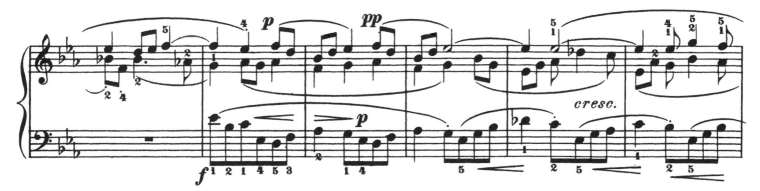

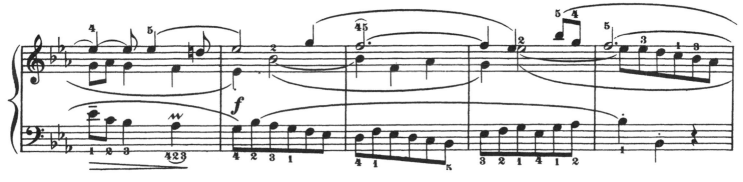

13212

XII.
Preludio.

Moderato assai. ($\quad$ = 52)

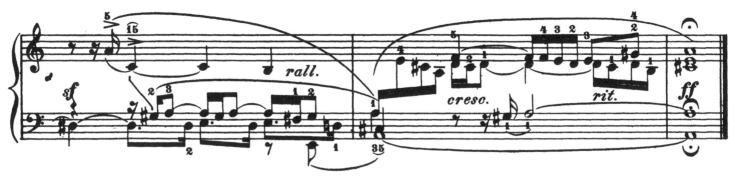

Fughetta.

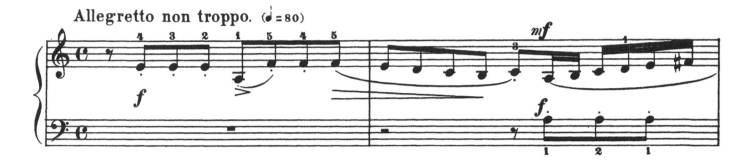

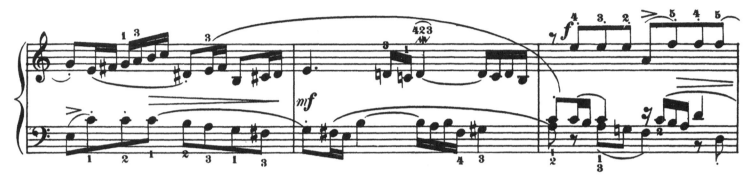

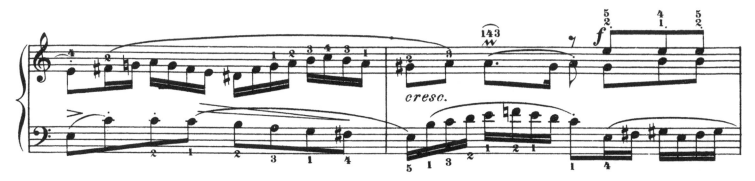

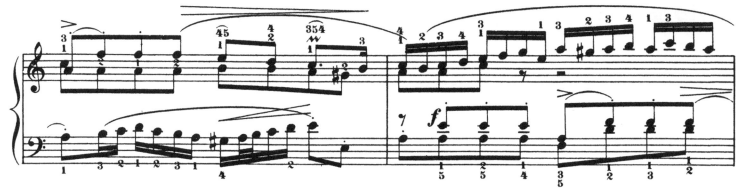

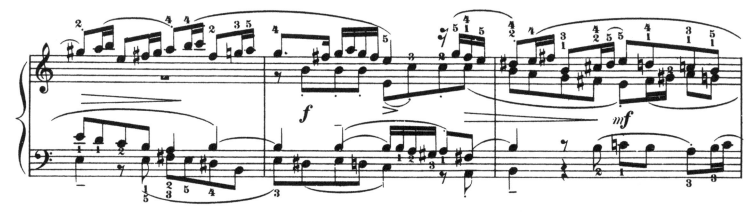

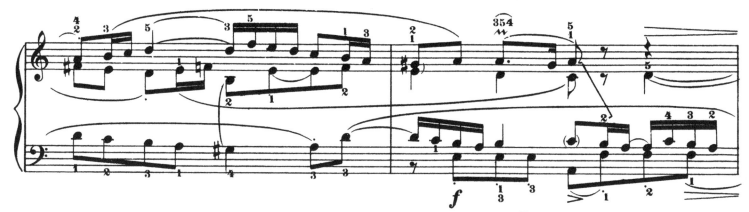

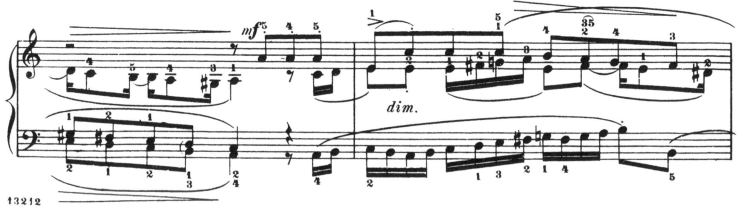

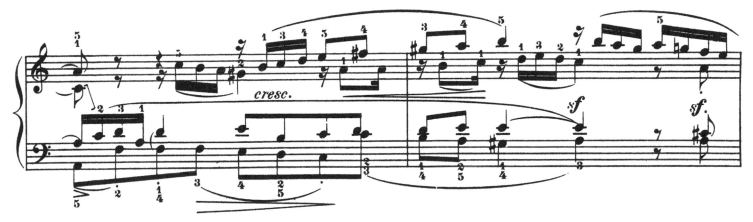

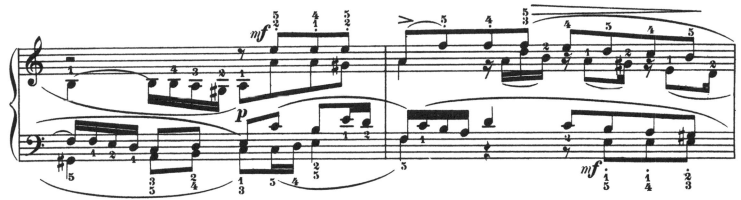

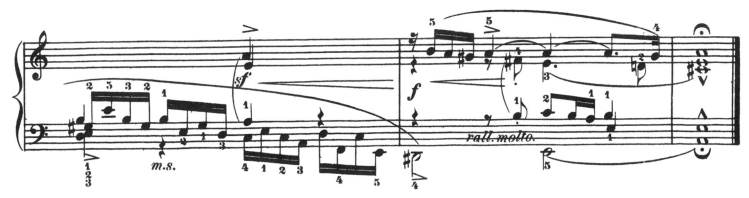

XIII.
Preludio.

Andante. (♩=76.)

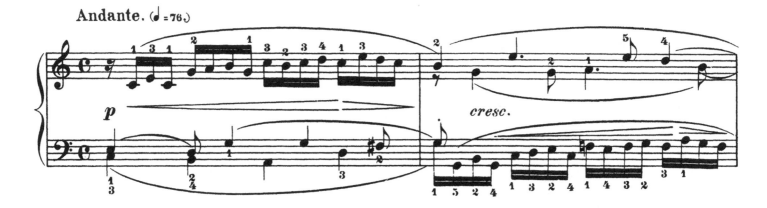

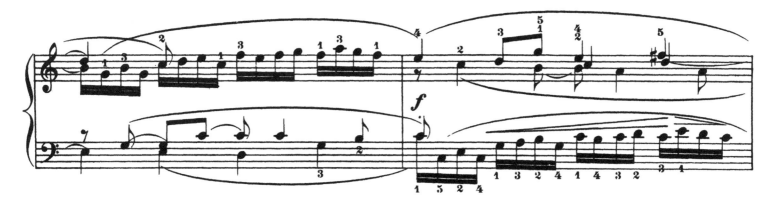

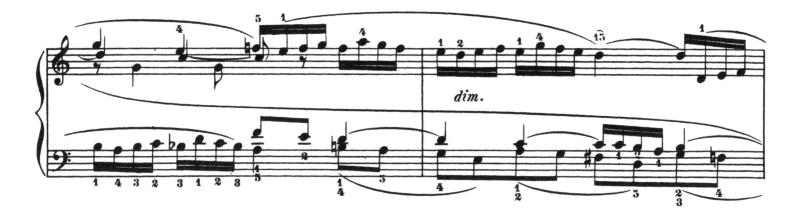

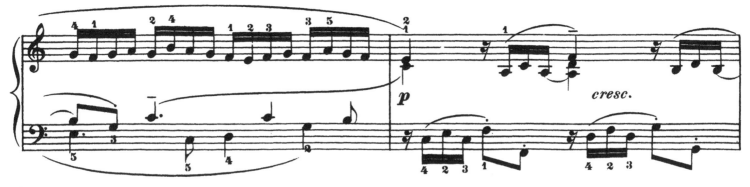

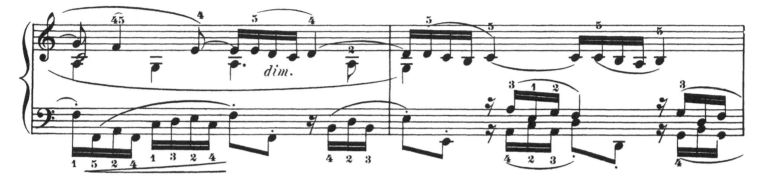

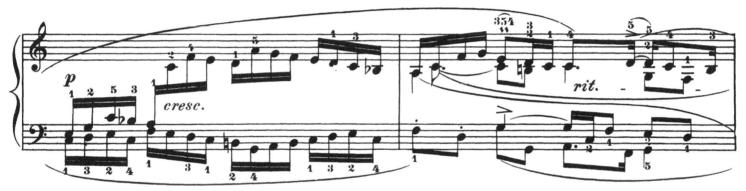

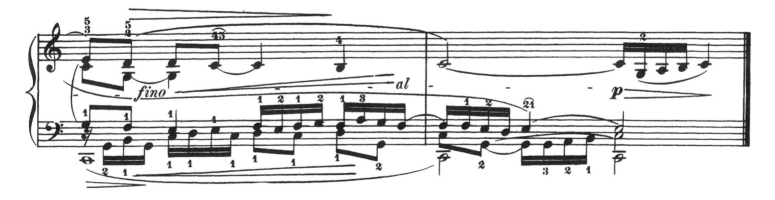

Fughetta.

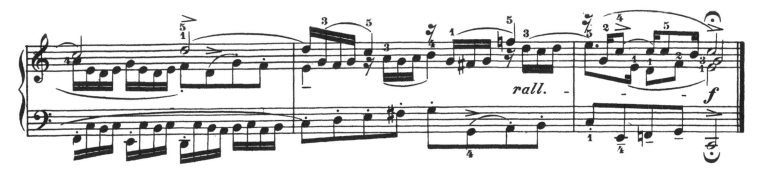

XIV.
Preludio.

Andante. ($\quad$ = 66.)

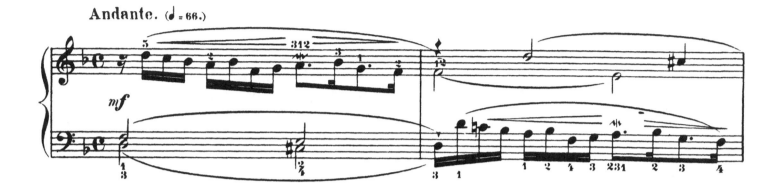

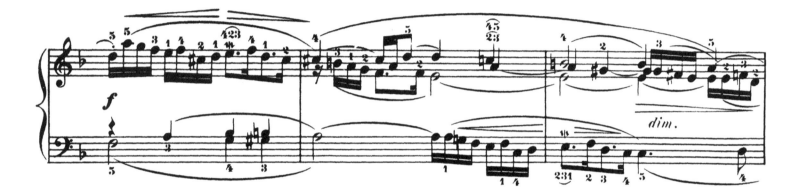

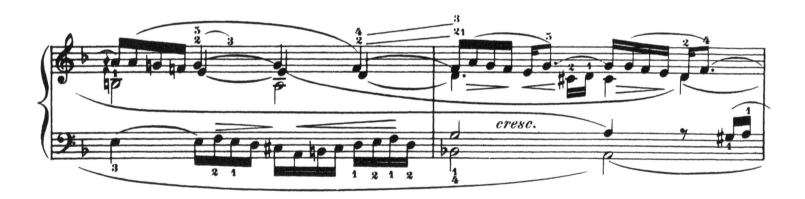

Fughetta.

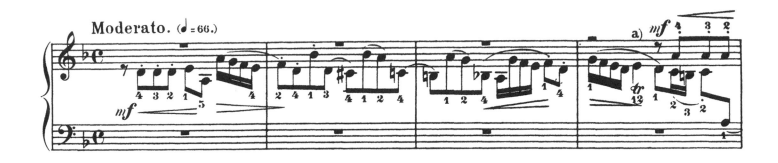

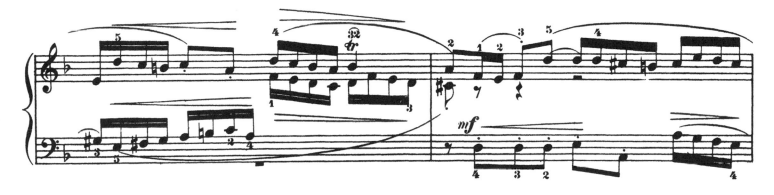

This fugue might have been the last in the collection, if its difficulty above had been considered; it is only because it is so short that I have given it a place here instead.

18212

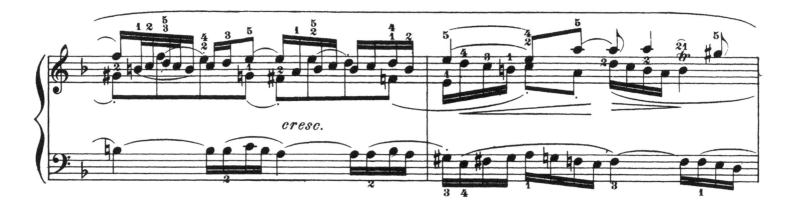

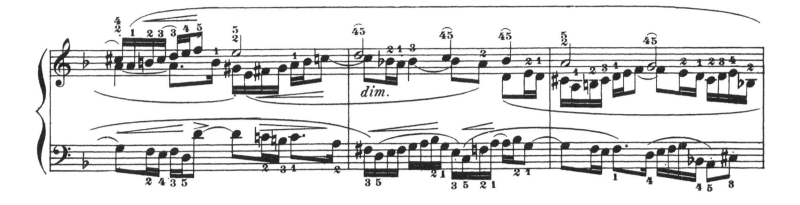

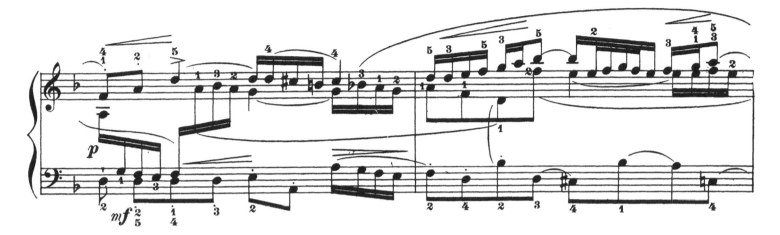

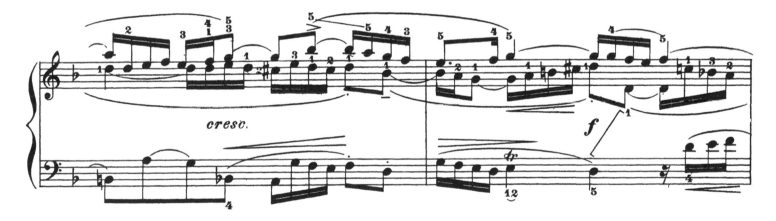

XV.
Preludio.

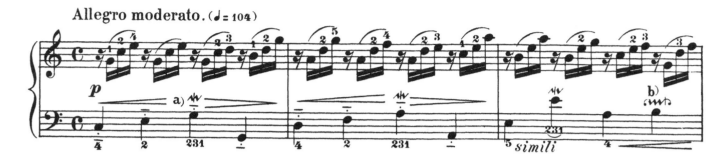

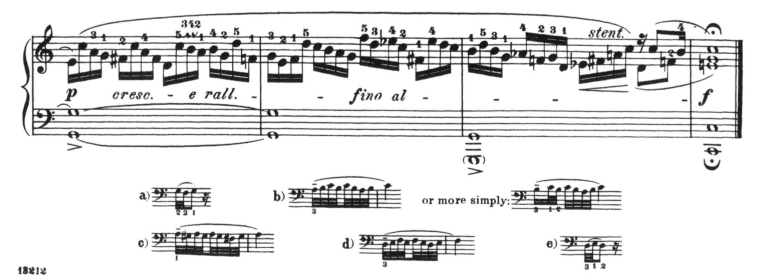

Fughetta.

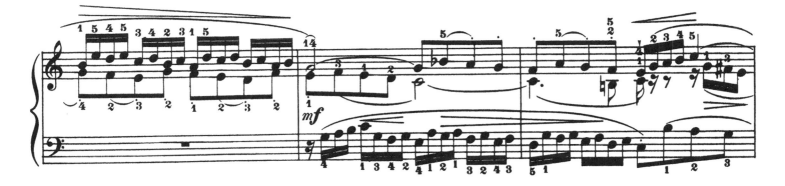

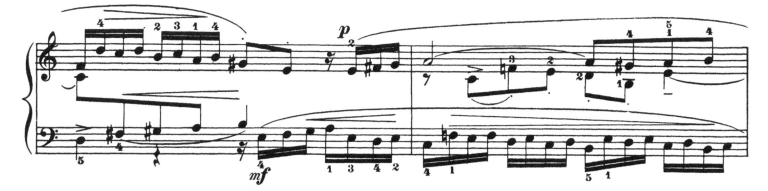

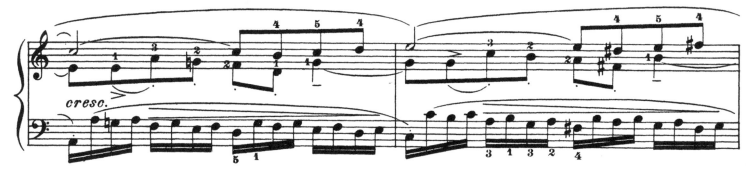

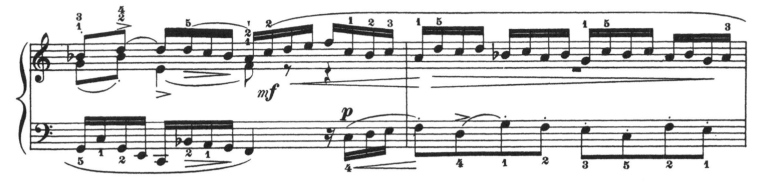

XVI.
Preludio.

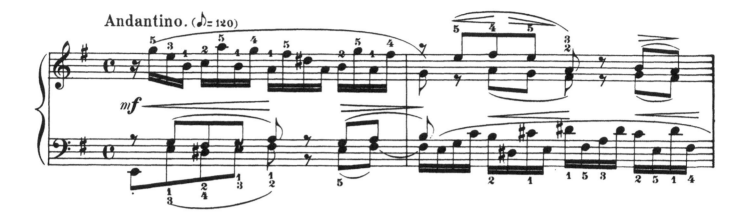

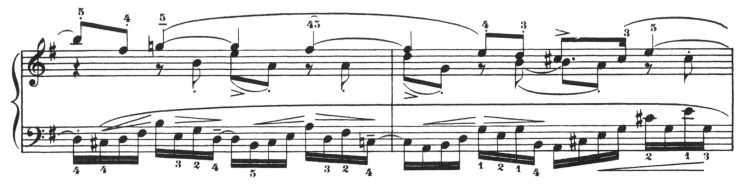

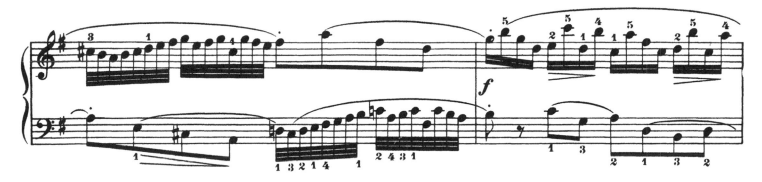

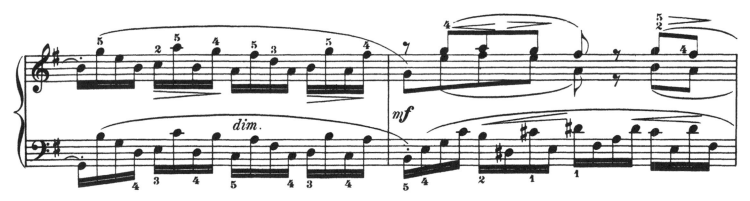

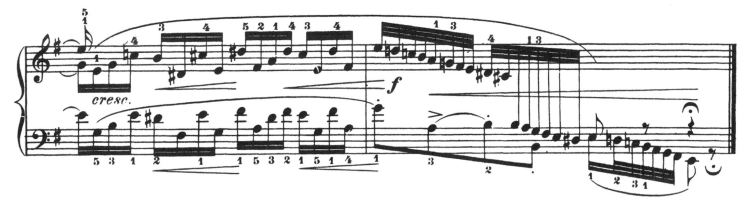

Fughetta.

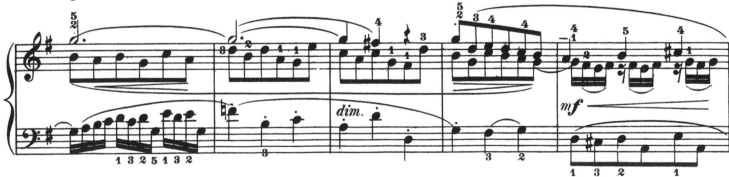

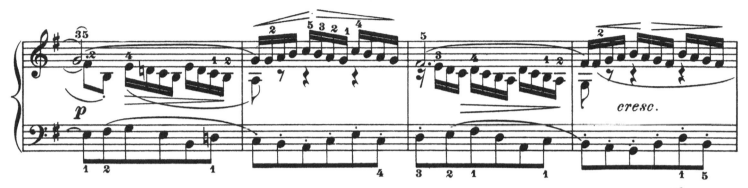

13212

XVII.
Preludio.

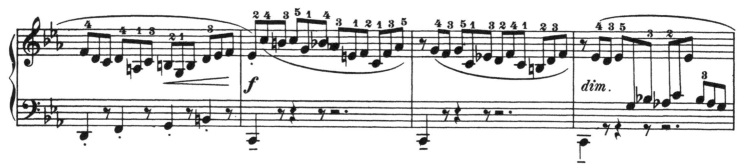

Fuga.

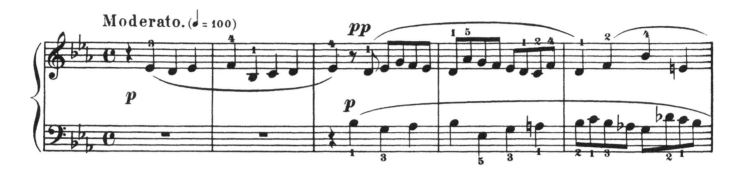

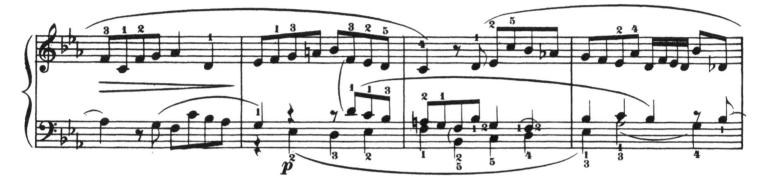

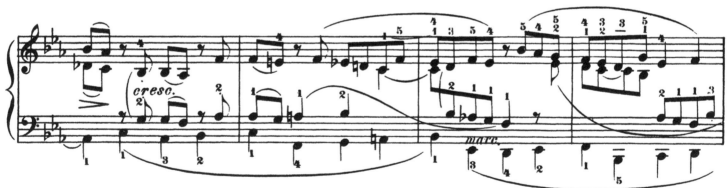

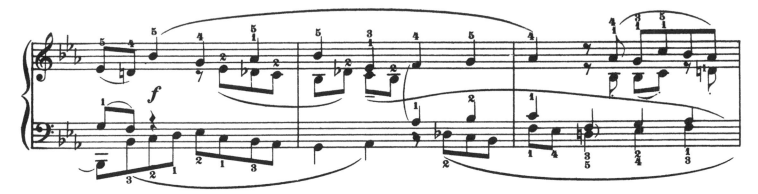

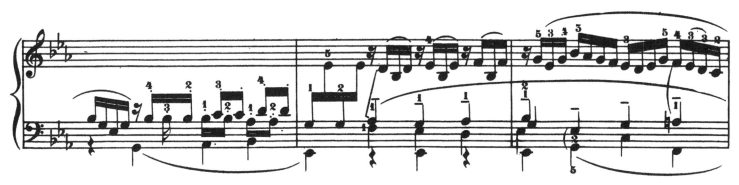

poco - - - a poco -

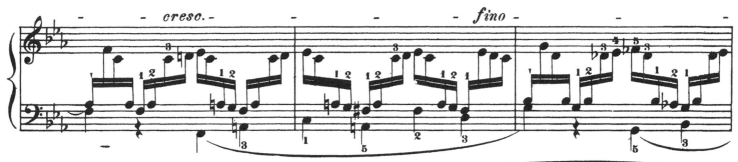

- - cresc. - - - - fino -

- - al - - - f

mf

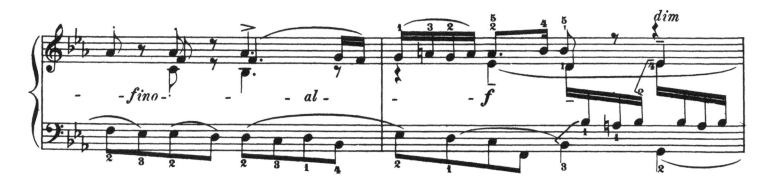

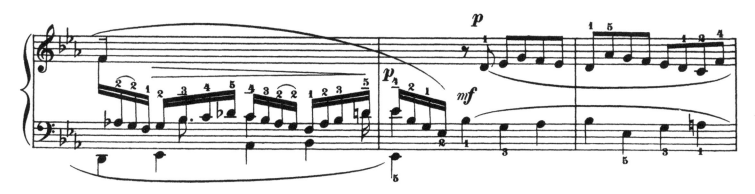

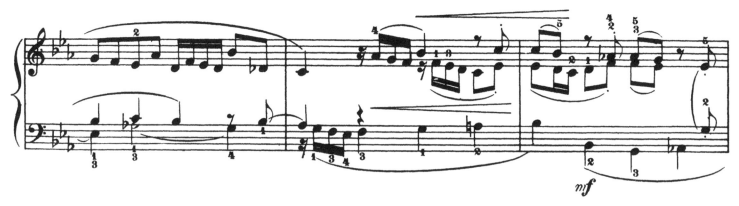

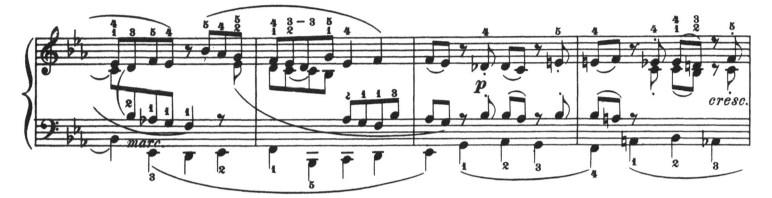

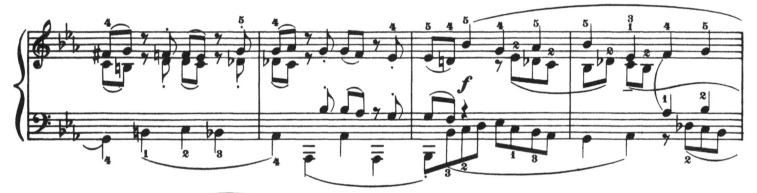

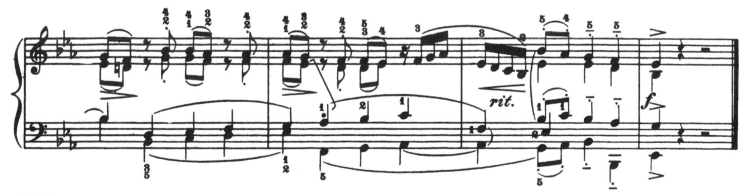

XVIII.
Preludio.

Allegro moderato. (♩. = 88.)

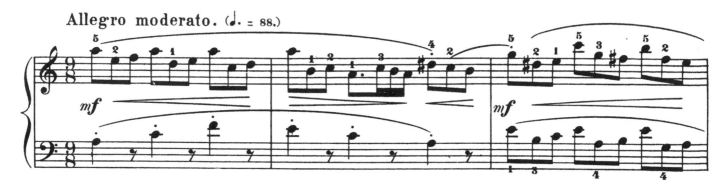

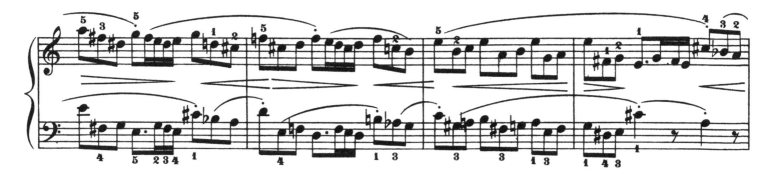

Fuga.

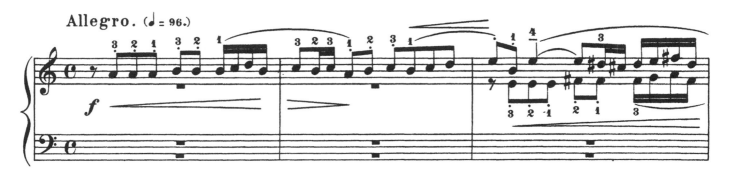

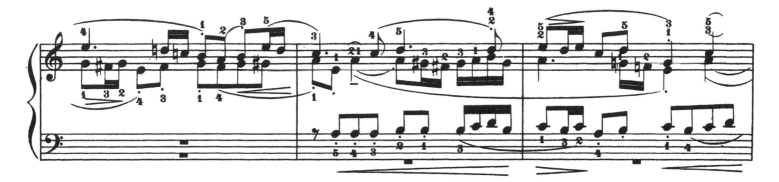

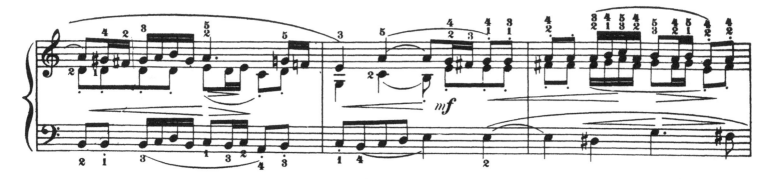

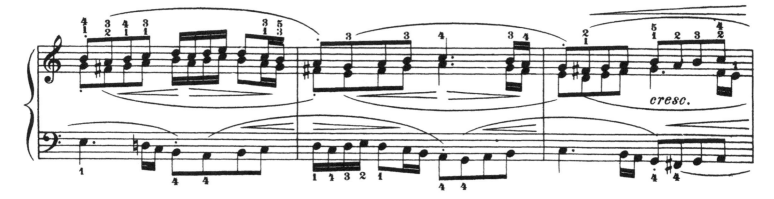

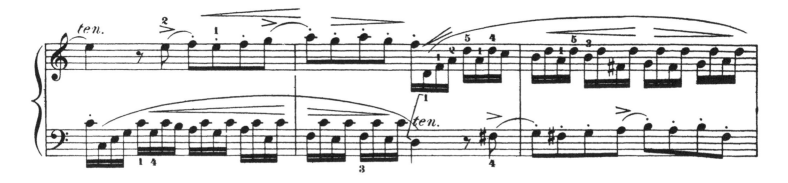

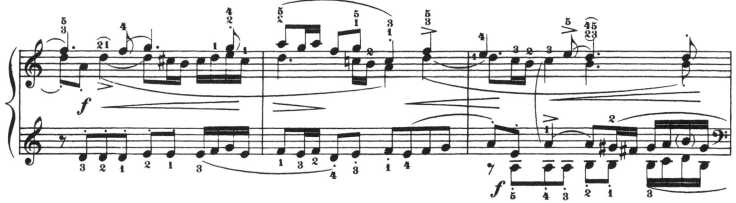

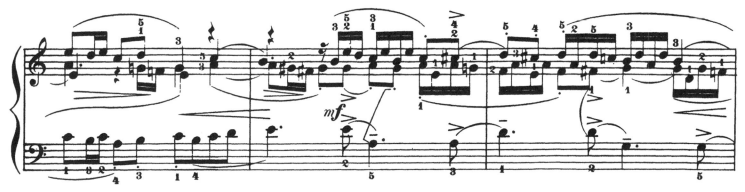

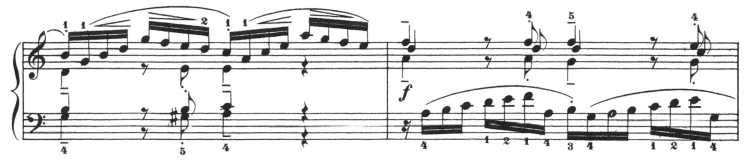

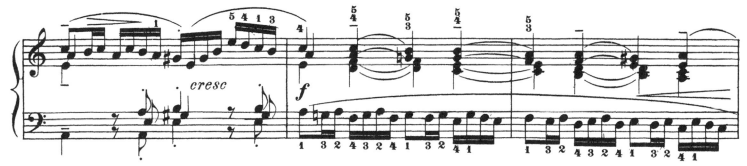

13212